The Bossy r
How the r Controlled Vowels Came to Be

by Lynell Hecht   illustrated by Alessyn Hecht

Copyright © 2016 by Lynell Hecht

All rights reserved. No part of this book may be reproduced, stored in a retrieval system, or transmitted by any means without the written permission of the author.

Printed in the United States of America

Written by Lynell Hecht

Illustrations by Alessyn Hecht

Graphic Design by Mike Bullard

First Printing, 2016

Version 1.0

ISBN 978-0-9973046-0-2

The Blessing Bell Company

Memphis, TN

www.LynellHecht.com

This book is dedicated to my husband, Paul, without whose support and encouragement, it would not have been completed.

Long ago,

before our **grandmothers** were even **born**, there were five **brothers** who lived up **north** on a **corn farm**. They did not live near anyone and were **far** from town. **Every Thursday**, they rode their **horses** into town to go to the **store** and **market**. They would get their supplies for the week, and that was the only time they got to see **other** people.

One **morning**, **after** a breakfast of **porridge** and **orange** juice, they could see **dark swirling** clouds **forming** off in the distance. They knew a bad **storm** was coming. They decided to work as **hard** and as fast as they could to get as much of their **corn harvested** so the **storm** would not damage their crop.

The **brothers** worked **harder** than they had **ever** worked. They did not even eat lunch. Finally, the **storm** was upon them. They put the **horses** and **rooster** in the **barn**, got their dog, and ran to the house for **cover**.

That night at **dinner**, they were exhausted. They were hungry. And they were **thirsty**. They were so tired, they could **hardly** lift a **finger**, much less lift a **fork** to their mouths.

The **corn** bread and **pork** chops were **burned**, so **dinner** was not as good as usual. The only thing they thought tasted good was their **dessert**... some **s'mores**.

Everybody was quiet. You could only hear the sounds of the **storm**. The lightning was bright, the **thunder** was loud, and the rain was pouring down. The wind was banging the **shutters** and **porch** swing against the house.

All of a sudden, there was a knock at the door! **Startled**, the **brothers** all sat up and looked at each **other**. The dog began to **bark** and growl. They **never** got visitors. Even on a beautiful day, they **never** got visitors. Who would be out in this kind of **weather**? And why were they knocking on THEIR door? They were all **nervous**... nobody wanted to **answer** it.

Finally, they decided to all **answer** the door **together**. One **brother** even carried his **fork**... just in case. The five **brothers** slowly opened the door. Now did you notice that these **brothers** were vowels? a,e,i,o, and u.

CREEEEEEEAK. They were not prepared for what was **before** them. In front of them stood the biggest, bossiest, ugliest, hairiest, and smelliest Bossy r they had ever seen!

Vowels a and o were so frightened that they **darted** out the back door, into the back **yard**, through the small vegetable **garden**, and down the path to the **barn**. Vowels e, i, and u just stood there. They were frozen with **surprise**.

The Bossy r raised his **arms** over the **brother** vowels and said, "From this day **forward**, you are all r controlled vowels! When you come before me in a word, you will make only my sound...the sound of a dog's growl...errrr (er, ir, ur)."

Then the Bossy r went to search for the **other** two vowel **brothers**. He went out the back door, into the back **yard**, through the small vegetable **garden**, and down the path to the **barn**. He **entered**, but the only things he saw were the **horses** and a **rooster**. Just as he **turned** to leave, a piece of hay floated down from the hayloft. He knew then that he had found the **other brothers**.

Bossy r climbed slowly up the **ladder**. He reached the top and looked around. **Over** in the **dark corner** were two lumps **under** the hay. He dusted the hay away from the **first** lump and there he was! The vowel a! The Bossy r raised his hands **over** the vowel and said, "You thought you escaped, but you didn't! From this day **forward**, you will be an r controlled vowel! When you come **before** me in a word, you will say the greeting of the pirate…argh (ar)."

He then moved **over** to the second lump. He dusted the hay away and **underneath** was the last vowel **brother**, the o! The Bossy r raised his hands over the vowel and said, "You thought you escaped, but you didn't! From this day **forward**, you will be an r controlled vowel! When you come **before** me in a word, you will make the sound of what the pirate uses to row his boat...Oar (or)!"

The vowel **brothers** still carry on happily to this day. At least one of them is in **EVERY** syllable of **EVERY** word in the English language. Even though the Bossy r is still bossy, they ended up becoming good friends. They work together in many words we say, read, and write every day. But, ever since that day long ago, when they are with the Bossy r in a word, we call them r controlled vowels (er, ir, ur, ar, and or).

And that is the story of how the r controlled vowels came to be!

The End

ABOUT THE AUTHOR

An educator for over 20 years, Lynell Hecht has always enjoyed coming up with ways to help make learning fun. The story, *The Bossy r*, is one of those ways. She also likes to throw the occasional ninja star. Really.

Lynell lives in Memphis, TN with her husband, two sons, and two cats.

www.ingramcontent.com/pod-product-compliance
Lightning Source LLC
Chambersburg PA
CBHW041128300426
44113CB00003B/99